LIGHT HERE, LIGHT THERE

Copyright © 2009 by Alexander Long

Printed in the United States of America

First Edition

ISBN 10: 0-9815010-6-0
ISBN 13: 978-0-9815010-6-2
LCCN: 2008943772

C&R Press
PO Box 4065
Chattanooga, TN 37405

www.crpress.org

For Julie,
With hope for our work.
—Alex

2 FEB '10

LIGHT HERE, LIGHT THERE

ALEXANDER LONG

Acknowledgments

Thank you to the editors of the following magazines and journals in which some of these pieces first appeared, sometimes in different versions:

13 Miles from Cleveland: "Kissing Lesson," "For the Girl in the Second Row"

580 Split: "After Andrew Wyeth's *Whale Rib*"

The Madison Review: "Dr. Kevorkian's Statement to Michigan's Superior Court as Prepared by Democratic Gubernatorial Candidate Geoffrey Fieger"

The Montserrat Review: "Meditation on Acceptance," "St. John's Extract"

Paragraph: "Love, Song"

Poemeleon: "Meditation on Anxiety," "Meditation on Denial & Isolation," "On Two Scenes from *The Deer Hunter*"

The Prose Poem: An International Journal: "Meditation on a Suicide"

Quarter After Eight: "Note to Self," "Objective-Subjective Exercise: I," "Objective-Subjective Exercise: II"

Quarterly West: "Meditation on Preparatory Depression"

Slipstream: "The Girl Smelling of Patchouli in the Bar Car"

Third Coast: "Noise"

Whirligig: "The Undertaker Preparing His Mother"

"Meditation on a Suicide," "Meditation on Denial & Isolation," "Meditation on Preparatory Depression," "Stepping into Poetry," "On Two Scenes from *The Deer Hunter*," and "Meditation on Acceptance" appear in the chapbook *Six Prose Poems*, Brandenburg Press, 2004.

Thanks to Chris Buckley, Fleda Brown, William Olsen, Beth Bachmann, Kate Northrop, Curtis Bauer, Marie Harris, and Sebastian Matthews for their critical eyes and generous support. Special thanks, always, to Marina Fedosik, and to my family.

Table of Contents

I

II

III

We live in two landscapes, as Augustine might have said,
  One that's eternal and divine,
                    and one that's just the backyard...

—Charles Wright, "Indian Summer"

I

So What

My father, after repairing triple-load washers for twelve hours on a Saturday, would put on Miles Davis' *Kind of Blue* and call me into the garage. "Hear this, slugger? One four five. That's all there is. Sons o' bitches...." I never understood how any man could be on his back for twelve hours and come home to listen to Miles Davis for another three. We split Budweisers. "So What" always on. I remember it that way. He sang the words that Miles didn't need. I was ten, eleven. The sun still out. Coltrane fading in after Miles' solo, then Miles gone. Gone for most of the song. He's not allowed to come back until the end. Those are the rules. That's the thing: my father taught me this. The rhythm section the whole time keeping time like running water. Brush stroke, snare off, over and again. Coltrane catches the wind of the last phrase, echoes, and goes wherever it was he went off to: Paradise, fishing with a cooler full, the driveway spotted with oil, the gear grease on his glasses and collar, the grease in his hair glinting blue at his wake, "So What" instead of a sermon.

Scar Tissue

Forty-ninth and Chester, cheap light-blue fluorescent lights, dusty ceiling fans swimming up more dust, cracked flood-worn floor, musty mop top in the washboard sink, Lou working graveyard shift for my father's father, then my father. Let me show you, as Lou did, the long skinny corridor behind the dryers, the thick rusty-looking gas pipes that run the floor every three feet. Give me your hand and let me show you how easy it is to trip, to burn your arms and hands on the pipes in front of us. Now, lie down like I am, next to me, look over me at how Lou's inside one like a mechanic, half-in, half-out: boot, sock, shin, pant, how he seems to ignore us...Do you see the twin scars on his shin, dark pink rings inches apart, shiny and smooth skin held in place, no nerves glowing where hair refuses to come back? Take my hand. I want you to circle the numb wounds, I need you to feel the nothing inside too.

READING KEES

1976, dusk, a family on the beach. My father stokes the fire, cracks another beer. My mother closes her book unmarked, and across the waves gulls turn orange against an orange moon. I see the lives of lovers, unmapped, unmarred by children—Father home from war, all biceps and jokes, Mother reciting Shakespeare: *Love is not love...and this gives life to thee*—five years ago, strolling in New Hope. How can I know them? My black lab digs a hole next to mine. I'm building a castle at high tide. Four years old. Dusk, a family on the beach.

FOR THE GIRL IN THE SECOND ROW

Like you, I have this image of my father in front of me, and every detail matters, swells: the snow gathering lazily, flake-by-flake, on the mallards' backs, their indifference to it that almost makes me bitter, younger, revisable, not like my father, who has become one of the old men I'll never see again on this blue park bench overlooking a lake, whose name I've always gotten wrong, a little beard of snow along its muddy edges.

Here is where I no longer believe that time is anything but one long exhalation.

His stare is a blank of sky reflected in the pond, his eyes distant, pink dusk, his hands as slow as the icicles above him in the sighing birches, hands that, Friday nights, would press a double bass to his chest and thump "A Night in Tunisia" till dawn, bow the dolor back into "Autumn Leaves," hands that taught me to do the same so I might hear our name in a clear unchanging voice.

One day, he thought once, he would stop staring and walk into the lake, slowly, to return to all he was, without choice or chance, born into becoming.

And this is the day my voice changed.

I first heard it in the way I was reading Stevens to my students.

Instead of praising what had, suddenly, been there all along, how sun and wave lilted *the woman striding there alone*, or how *the figures in the street / Become the figures of heaven*, it was my father wading there, then vanishing in my voice inflected by many waves, and ice.

I'm trying to explain. I mean, whatever I had to say about time, my father, a name, a voice, made a girl in the second row wince as she fixed her perfect hair. When I looked at her all I could see were tiaras of snow collecting on the ice of a lake he's walking into until time, too, loses its breath, a wind barely moving at all.

I see it now, and can you hear it, now? This is my voice.

My student, she was, like me I guess, learning the cold, the light it drops, how hydrangeas bulge fully blue, how acres of corn sweeten perfect spines, how this is all decoration for the body turning toward water.

Anna, may your dream not be the wandering kind of a father moving through ice and water, gently, humming a tune not yet thought up, the mallards shaking snow off their green and gorgeous heads, the birches' icicles extending in their dissolution, like his image and name are doing just now.

HOLDING LARRY LEVIS' PEN

—for Phil, Franny, and Bruce

I hear three, maybe four voices weaving through each other. They vanish, begin, and vanish like smoke into light. I am told this is the pen he held as he rose from an elegy to get some water before he fell into elegy. I am told that the pen has traveled from Utah to Yugoslavia, Rome to Richmond, Frankfurt to Fresno, that for its last journey someone took the care to wrap it in a red handkerchief with white embroidery—*L P L*—then wrapped it in stories from the *Richmond Times-Dispatch*, seeds for the memoirs of battles to come, case histories of molestation and abuse; that it traveled with an old wine box filled to the top with sheets of paper, poems finished and unfinished and infinite, a heap of elegies a trusted friend moved through slowly with the pen. One voice rises above the others, and as he looks at me his voice changes, slightly, and it feels as though he's speaking through me and directly to himself. I'm forbidden to share what was said, but I'm told that I may hold the pen, a simple Parker 51, empty cartridge, new nib. I remove the cap and trace something invisible, present.

On a Meeting of Philip Levine and Larry Levis

*...let's not
invent a dialogue of such eloquence
that even the ants in your own
house won't forget.*
> —Levine

*...so that
You won't mistake him for something else,
An idea, for example...*
> —Levis

Fresno, September 30, 1996, Larry's once and future 50th birthday, and, of course, he is the shit-grinning angel smoking on Phil's front porch; of course, he's got an all-too-clear idea of the elegies that will curse and bless him, contemptible hymns dressed up as grief. The young man who tried to bring them together hasn't the guts to knock on Phil's front door, and paces his side yard lined with roses. He realizes, now, too late, that he has no business doing this, and is out of smokes, and bites his nails to blood. For a moment's relief he sits on the curb to catch his breath, visible now at night. Something catches in it, an eternal vision of such grief he has to press his arms across his chest to keep from rising.

Let's not be pretentious, nor witty, not political. Let's be sentimental, let's simply put them back together, because, as with all elegies, this has everything to do with *me*. The two greatest influences one might have, and what happens? A man, turning 24 in two days, throws up on Philip Levine's curb.

Have you ever gotten sick, I mean so sick you shook and swore you cracked a rib, the upper most left one, and jerked back at the vision of your father weeping on the steps of his first house, not because he's lost it, but because it's his with you in it? A house like all the others, surrounded by airplanes, and the dust of airplanes bound for Fresno, Richmond, Detroit, Barcelona? Have you ever risen from bed and tiptoed to the screen door, peered through its top half with holes that moths drift through, seen him hunched on his own steps? Oh, yes, let's write this down because you're not allowed to be up this late. Let's put him right here in front of us so we don't mistake him for anything else, an elegy, say, for someone we nearly knew. Phil, brushing his teeth and humming happy birthday before he brings down the lights; and Larry, stepping on his always-next-to-last cigarette, would remind you of that.

In Memory of William Matthews

I.

His mind danced for pure pleasure. Nothing more human than that, for pleasure is, as Freud said, "what we are ignorant of."

He had no false regrets, as far as I can tell.

His poetry makes nothing whimper.

In his mind, Mingus and the Babe shook hands, we snickered at divorce and time, and always the pun he loved at the end of a mouth of merlot.

He rose and fell. Dawn would come.

The poets of New York and altogether elsewhere, now that he is scattered among a hundred cities, giggle and cry.

II.

They're always riffing on eternity, the masters. Always the tonal heart.

But Mingus throws his pianist out for improvisational reasons anyway, soothes the crowd, and begins again the body of work that's made him expansive and difficult.

A line is implied by how his callused hands make the silence fall as long as we're listening.

The clenched, callused hand can be cruel.

PROPOSAL

Eight years ago this August, I woke in a sweat, grabbed both of her hands, and asked her to marry me. She turned and mumbled, draped her leg onto mine, and fell back asleep.

I can only speak of her steady breath for hours, of the first light by our open bedroom door.

THE SUN RISES IN THE EAST

Eight years since, and all I can see is sunset, sunset, sunset, and my ex father-in-law walking with me a long way up a small mountain named after his family.

Now what?

Now he's leading the way, not saying a word, the moment after I tell him his daughter and I are ending things, and here's my ex mother-in-law spooning stuffing onto my plate, saying *Helluva time—Christmas, then New Year's—to be breaking up, that's just great, what will I tell the church elders and my bridge club...,* and here's my ex laughing before she actually starts crying, but only to herself.

I knew her that well then.

Eight years, and I'll forgive myself this once for poking at my plate like a five-year-old, for ending up at the table by myself. I'll forgive Time for making it happen between Christmas and New Year's. I'll bless my abandoned imagination for remembering, for having to, for never telling why.

Today I'll write, "Good people, my ex in-laws. Fed me, even set up a couch I could lie on a few hours before I ducked out, before sunrise, while their daughter slept in the bed she had as a child, in the room with two windows facing east."

MEDITATION ON ANXIETY

It comes from the slightest shift in light or from one cigarette
too many or from too much or not enough bourbon or from
Wolf Blitzer and Dick Cheney and Karl Rove or from checking
my bank statement or from a broken air conditioner in August
or from that random memory I had today—not even a memory,
really, but more a fraction of an image—a flash of a shelf-less
curio with mirrors for its insides my ex and I trash-picked
in Michigan seven, eight years ago and tried to clean up and
used as a centerpiece in our living room to make it look bigger
before she moved out and all the old shards of childhood
resurfaced in torrents of guilt and long of bursts of regret and
muffled bouts of crying before, during, and after my trips to
the shrink. The strangest thing, that half-flash, that fractal of
an image: no people, no sound, hardly no setting at all, just
white walls, sheer curtains caught in mid-billow, the curio's
glass doors and mirrored insides and faux mahogany finish
there. Undeniably there, centered and unmovable. Neither of
us wanted it anymore. For weeks, we'd negotiated who would
get what: she the couch, me the coffee table, she the bed, me
the TV, she two cats and the dog, me the other two cats, she
the car payments, me the credit cards, she the Tiffany lamp,
me the signed hardback of Wright's *This Journey*, she the grief
and guilt, me the grief and guilt. The curio stood there in the
corner of the empty living room—I remember this distinctly,
she standing there and me standing there, our arms folded,
the two of us standing there, a new distance—looking at it, at

us, and what to do, what to do, what to do, the sound of a foot tapping, multiple exposures of us inside the three mirrored walls of the curio, the shapes of light careening and shifting. I wanted this poem to be more than a re-telling, more than a complaint, admission. I wanted to move beyond—or at least understand—the faint pitch and frequency of what I remember and why. I wanted to talk with you, maybe help you out a little, and help myself out a little. I wanted to document one of those fractious images that seem to matter because it keeps shining and shifting until it can't not be seen, denied. I didn't want to end up staring into a curio again, shifting foot-to-foot, speechless, arms folded, walking finally into another room. That curio must still be standing somewhere, reflecting whoever is front of it.

FROZEN

In Philly, the blizzard of '96 dumped three feet of snow on our sprawling suburban-subdivision-development. I'd been shoveling out the wrong car for about two hours when George, my neighbor—57, on crutches from a skiing accident that involved a stroke—saw me. I was almost done, freezing in my knees, socks stiff, goatee glittering with crystal breath. His car was over *here*, not the one *there*, why didn't I ask first, *I'm a good kid, goddamnit, but I should've asked, shit it's cold out here, get in here for a toddy, Jameson's and lemon, I won't take no....*

Noon, a toddy, a Saturday, I didn't want to waste any more time because what we know, what we think we know, what we ask for is merely all we can remember to keep the brain calm until it decides to still itself without warning while the heart goes on pulsing the rest of the body along, reassuring it that all is well, suspending the anguish of a terrifying jolt whose obsession is stillness, not unlike the way we nurture the tiny thousands of denials of the day in the daylight world of the living with drink and song and love, which pass through us, leave us....

George had one those long slivers of smoothed glass for a stirrer. It chimed against the mugs. We watched playoff football for hours on his big screen TV, talked about nothing the way good friends do and don't feel awkward, talked about the absence of women—his wife in New Mexico three years now, the recent passing of his mother, daughter starting her first year up at Penn State. His words slightly slurred—*I know my life is real now...*—an offering that meant a life, the conversation stilled, the huge unified sound of the crowd cheering from the television, our blank stares turning toward it.

SNOW SHOWER WITH SUN

Right now I'm sipping coffee, thinking about you, how we once kissed on Church Street, how the cold suddenly disappeared as stars hovered in their glass coats then came in close to catch a glimpse because they know that first kisses stop time every time; and when I lift the cup to wake in the world where you are, I look up at this sky shining, turned on, blinding, a rush of pink and gold and white, a flowing hush ocean-sized where a young girl and her mother close their eyes and catch crystals on their tongues.

KISSING LESSON

A flick of the hair and she secures my hand to hers, leans in, backs away, leans in, "No, like this...." So. May God's string of pearls called stars unravel like a dime-store rosary, like the perfect run-on sentence slipping through our lips, may her mouth always be mine, may our wordless, timeless prayer carry out its work in our deeds all the rest of our days, may this undiscovered cosmos flushed with breath rise and rise and rise, may we feel an end to nothing.

FIREFLIES AT MIDNIGHT

A cool June night in the hammock, I spill some wine down your shirt, you bite my neck, and as we fumble onto our backs grabbing and twitching, a flicker above us, another, then another, but it's not just that God-blown glass called Cassiopeia, her swaying *W* on Milky Way's fringe; no, it's a school of fireflies scattering their perfect affection, a pearl necklace of couplings to come, a flash of flesh of what we could be, what we might call *breathless* or *ecstasy* or *beauty*; it mystifies science because what they don't understand is that beauty is not something to be solved but entered, like your green eyes widening, your mouth opening with the first word of a new day borne by this light dropped unconditionally, without which we'd be lost, which we are—and are not— swaying in our new-found lightness.

II

AT THE TROLLEY STOP

Sometimes I want to go back and walk all day with her, sleep sitting on a bench next to her. Sometimes I'm glad I can't go back at all.

It seems pointless now to tell you what she looked like, but once in the parking lot by the SEPTA 102 stop in Sharon Hill, this woman I'd see every day was trying to add things up, I guess. All she had was time in those silver trash bags and granny cart, so she yanked up her coat, squatted down, and took a piss. A teenage girl looked on, trying to shield her baby's eyes.

I felt little. The present is like that.

I remember steam rising from the asphalt.

When she pulled up her pants, her coat flapped like Old Glory itself. Oh Washington. Oh Lincoln. Oh Kennedy. I love my town and I'm still young. In Sharon Hill, the sun comes up a little; and after it moves on from the sea of lights and huddled circles of gamblers in Atlantic City, it touches the exploded panes that line the houses.

Whitman walked there. Bessie Smith is buried there.

But the buses won't run there anymore. If you want to get

someplace, you've got to use the two feet God gave you.

So, she looked into the sky and breathed in the salty savor of her piss that, if she thought about it, might resemble whatever's next to nothing.

The thought would hold if she wanted it to.

She said nothing, and there wasn't a thing I could do but stare at her steam that offered a little more gray to the afternoon. The teenage mother mumbled something predictable to herself—"That dusty old" or "That is so sick...." The woman didn't have to hear it. She grabbed her cart and began her walk up Chester Pike. Clouds passed overhead. I warmed some coins with my breath in my hands, tender that used to get me out of there.

Air Ball

1981, late March or early April, and who cares when it happened. It happened. I was nine, holding court at the free throw line, sleet-drizzle ticking off my Coke-bottle bifocals—Kurt Rambis a hero, had I been from L.A.—dribbling the ball three times, one for the Father, one for the Son, one for the Holy Ghost, and...air ball. Never good or gritty enough to make the CYO squad from Holy Spirit. One court over, Jamaal, Bodie, Theopholous-Thomas, and Ronnie, big Black Men who could kill the rim from above, could double-pump mid-air, then raise the ball from their waists and hang from the rim, tongue-wagging...all pre-Jordan, all twenty-some years ago, all Sharon Hill, all race and rage and Reagan recouping, all ice-rain in late March or early April, all of us spread out across two courts. From beyond the makeshift arc—a crack in the asphalt—they'd make the chains sing *swish* whenever they wanted. God, hear me: they would.

During, between, and after their 2-on-2s on a half court, I'd catch snatches of them trash-talking each other into stitches—"all them bricks, you moms get a new house; I'm Hinckley—Bang!—but I finish that job; bitch, don't be laughing, you next"—all the I-Love-Yous-as-Fuck-Yous, the necessary etiquette of survival on courts with chains for nets, cracks as borders. The greatest insult was *not* to get dressed down, and I was needing them to consider my air ball—I know why now—as they sat there, maybe watching me, maybe sipping on something in a soaked brown paper bag, toking on something that might've cut through the icy rain and rage and history, the feel of it all landing in small slivers—the weight of a cat's shed claw—on our heads and hands. They said nothing, not even the easiest trash, *Nothin' but the bottom of the net....* They knew that was too easy. They must have. They left me alone.

ON EDEN

Every morning the sun on MacDade Boulevard hangs itself on the MacDade Mall's marquee advertising, three years now, "Al Raymond's Good Time Oldies Band." If you turn left, you can make out Liberty Place and William Penn staking their claim in the fog. If you turn to the right and wait, you'll smell the Amish carrying the wood and manure of their chores to fire that by noon will blaze and boil the water to clean their shirts. For a second, as you light a smoke, you will try to embrace their discipline and belief, and finding it, you'll keep walking.

You have to keep walking.

If you're not from Philly, this means little to you. You have only an idea of what I praise.

But listen: light a candle and place it in the center of your table. Ignore the neighbors to your left, the young couple married last March, who throw insults and bottles and plates at each other.

Nod *Good morning* each morning to Ethel on your right, who bakes an apple pie each week, who is, at once, sweet and one with the land.

Sit in a red, white, and blue lawn chair and curse its rust that stains your good white shirt. Count the seven little American flags lining your plot of grass. And every Fourth of July, walk with your boy through Darby and Collingdale, Boston and Modesto, to watch the sky explode.

Distant Reader, are you with me?

This *is* about you, for you.

You have to hate where you are from. Otherwise, you'll smolder. Places, their names, will disappear before you every day, and you'll never know it. You'll long for Atlantic City, an oasis as dry as birch bark in a driveway. You'll forget your dreams of Stockholm in June, of Prague in July.

You have to get yourself exiled for a crime you did not mean to commit; you have to deny it and accept it as you step on a cigarette on the courthouse's steps.

You have to pay your lawyer in kind, an "up yours" for a "you momma."

And you must accept, too, that all other ways fail.

Eat your pie, trace the fireworks for what they are.

All that matters is that you hold it up to your boy on your shoulders, and that you keep walking the boulevard as the moon lights your backs.

To the Girl Smelling of Patchouli Oil
in the Bar Car

Or maybe because back here we don't have much of a choice. Because you are as young as desire permits, an awkward silence sliding in behind you, where you are right now: exiled, with the rest of us clutching warm cans of Heineken.

Because your braided pigtails are purposefully thrown to almost hide your breasts, and because of the dabs of patchouli on your wrists and neck you will never step out of, your motionless feet, not one lick of Monk or Miles in you.

Because we listen to the men in the corner get louder talking boxing, the ethics of the left jab, one mad man biting another's ear half off, as if he were asked to, then their own stories, one after another, getting more and more ridiculous.

Because the Vietnam vet, who has no stories we haven't already heard, is so gone he can't see how the eyes and jawbone of the Korean student are Korean, and because the old woman is mumbling her one good idea of the day to herself between cigarettes and Pepsis with lime, *Gimme every American male doctor under 50 and I'll ship 'em off to Liberia, Iraq, Bosnia... sonsofbitches let me tell you...*maybe to attend to the splintered ghosts who are her grandparents, who are as unchanging as the need for violence itself.

I look into your hair, and the architecture of desire is the same wherever, no matter this limited set of reflections where, from my seat, I can see that I am next to you; and the vet and woman play a version of Crazy Eights not yet made up; the men laugh and wave in the air at things that are there and not there; and the Korean student reads his dictionary, practicing the answers to questions we no longer think to ask.

It is better this way, this distance we've acquired.

We haven't moved for hours, any of us.

Notes About Water

I.

This grass I've cut, not long ago, was sucking all it could from the earth. I ended all that. Now, spread in moist clumps over the sidewalk, it resembles islands in the South Pacific or atolls spun for nothing on the sweet blue wrap of ocean East Coast surfers dream about. Soon enough, those blades will leave each other, carried off as hay, simplified, and one step further, all the way to Purgatory, Kansas.

II.

Consider the fire at the group home for the disabled. While the house slowly undressed itself, those inside sat up in awe of the flames draping the windows. Water is what separates this life from the other ones. Maybe it's sunlight they felt as they slipped a little deeper into their skulls. I'm sure water sat cool and trembling in the pipes while cars glided over the road, the sizzle of tires sounding like waves to everyone else. After all this time, I wish I could think they were swooning to a Billie Holiday ballad—"Body & Soul" or "Solitude"—purring on the old phonograph, like in the movies.

III.

Here's my reflection in a puddle: all the metals and oils mixed with water that is flesh, but isn't. I'll cup my hands and gather it up. Look, there I am again, and again, falling back to earth.

ANOTHER POEM ABOUT LOSS (THINKING ABOUT TWA FLIGHT 800 FIVE YEARS LATER)

—July, 2001

The ocean lies flat, shines like plastic wrap on a pack of cigarettes, it's stuck in textbooks, and is never seen face to face, the way one might read about St. John, or his assassins the Gnostics never wrote about. For the old janitor, who continues to move at his glacial pace down those hallways, waxed smooth with light, the sky could be a scar reopened in the cradled web between his index finger and thumb. Say he's torn it on a rusty tin trashcan. Or it's a papercut that never bled. Either way, it's as memorable as The Act of Contrition, and because it's always July, there's no one in the hallway to guide him to the nurse's office for a Band-Aid or gauze, no one to remind him that his memory, like saltwater and sand, comes and goes with the tide. There's just the music of his feet shuffling across linoleum, the whine of the rope for the blinds, the light of some morning five years ago lazily filling each room. He grunts as he lifts the next or next-to-last desk, his back muscles shivering not like a thoroughbred's, not yet noticing how the room is suddenly more spacious.

I remember how relaxed I was that evening, on the patio, cool beer and breeze, ball game crackling through the transistor, a little lightning threatening nothing, and then the news from Long Island: plane down, all gone. Later, witnesses said *fireworks, one huge light, missiles, rock concert,* the past thrown to the future unwillingly and without fail, as it always is, as every apocalypse is personal. I looked into the sycamore where bats slept, and five years later I still want to say it looked beautiful as I listened, its rustling like heaved breath, a mist the color of dawn, which was suddenly there, uninvited, hovering between the sycamore and me before we all slipped toward the center of the world...

NOISE

It's the man in front of me half-turned around and staring, not the woman behind me whose voice controls her, summons those around her to turn and take notice for a second or two, those who'd care not to listen, those who have seen her before, know her, know what's coming, what she has and brings: small sounds from her nose; loud ones coughed up; murmurs shouted; cigarette-husk; throaty scats and half-words: *oh, ooh, yeah-yeah-yeah, uh-oh*; full sharp words: *eat, yes, now*; laughs that could be cries, cries that could be real, pain and joke overlapped and thrown together, encircled and sickled through her. The man looks at her, back at me, then down to his checkbook, squelches a chuckle, rolls his eyes, mumbles something to the cashier, particulars inaudible and hovering, and I could tell you that I chewed him out then and there, that I laughed along with him, exchanging barbs, cruel comfort; I could tell you that the woman lifted a clear and pointed *Fuck you* at the two of us, echo and swirl; I could talk about clarity and why it blossoms inviolably in everything outside us—couldn't I?—how it sounds like a cat clawing at the door, wind in the lindens, the ocean.

Love, Song

January, Philadelphia, 22nd and Fairmount, almost noon, and some guy waves a crumpled cup and tattered sign: DEAF NEED BUS FARE. Above, a littered sky wanting night too soon. Dark cars glide through slush, brights on, little orange funeral flags on the hoods. I want to press *pause* and drift into pines weighed with snow, our cottage closer, its fogged windows overlooking tracks in snow that lead to the door, your hands taking my hat and gloves, you pressing your hand to my cheek. Tea bags steep, a steaming kettle calms. You're someone to stir the sugar, someone to stir the sugar in for...Let me drift, let me...Then, again, you're gone. I turn up the radio. Through the car's speakers Hendrix's "Manic Depression" swells swiftly, each line slicing through the one before it, wind over ice. To hell with it. I curse this block plowed in by a funeral. I curse. I curse this guy who bangs my window with his sign. I curse the mourners, glacial in their grief. I curse Hendrix, wicked and bright and on.

After Andrew Wyeth's *Whale Rib*

I.

Dear Mr. DePaul, I've got a secret to tell you. We can remember
the parts of the conversations that never happened. You're
thinking of your son again, aren't you? You'd have named
him Hank Junior, you're thinking, and what stays behind
your eyes is something I wouldn't see for twenty years: a scene
Andrew Wyeth has grown old in: Maine, hunched in the sand,
wave spume blue, brown brush, slivered silver-white whale
rib about forty feet in shore.

Only you saw it different. Tell it again, how you trudge over
the Isle of Wight. Post-recon, right? *Who was going to pick
that thing up and put it there? I can't hardly see it now ... I
didn't have no camera then. Weren't allowed.* Was it smooth
as teeth or bumpy like a tree branch? How'd it get there?
*Don't know. German torpedo sub, bombs my unit dropped,
the moon. The landmine holes big as tractor tires, my dog
tag sack clicking, we called it "walk-and-fall, trip-and-walk,"
humming "String of Pearls," "April in Paris," "Stardust..."*
fear a passage into fear, fearing passage, close-mouthed.

II.

This has also happened: in Cedar Rapids, Iowa, a screen door
is blown off its hinges. Inside, a woman at a desk craves a

cigarette after she's ripped up the letter that's taken her four months to write. She doesn't smoke. It's to her sister, a nun working in Hell's Kitchen. *This fucking wind* and *All men are goddamned liars* and *I'll tell you what that little bastard went and did*...She doesn't talk like this, think like this. But there it is and it is 1943, the Heartland, a woman living alone, her sister tending new sheep, her brother beginning his apprenticeship as a fossil in the side of a Sicilian mountain.

III.

Celan advises: "listen your way in / with your mouth." He, for example, listened his way to the Seine littered with light.

IV.

My sister told me over drinks how the bottle killed Mr. DePaul. He loved the Civil War, Dewars, and German Shepherds. Once, my mother let him take me two hours west to Gettysburg with Gretchen Number Two, one of those all-black German Shepherds. I can't imagine back the quiet ride in the car enough, frozen air blackening the windshield, Gretchen twitching with sleep in the back, talk radio fading to static, then snow. I was maybe eight, no fear. I remember the wart on his nose and the star-shaped divot-scar on his lower right jaw. *Indian pegged me with an arrow. I yanked it out, and kept on firing. Purple Heart. Dee-dee-dee, dah-dahhhhh....* "April in Paris." He told good stories: whale rib, Indians, the arrow. *You tell good stories,* is what I told him.

V.

"The power and the horror of the raging sea," Wyeth says. He's got it: the sea, far off in the upper left-hand corner fades into its own reflection, becomes sky, then canvas. Closer to shore, the water slams and bangs itself over the beach's cliff. It's all over him, violence etched into fear. "Thrilling!" he says. The whale rib is sharp, tapered, ragged, like an old knife, pocked by rust. I can't decide how heavy it is, how much fury it would take for me to throw it back whence it came, how many salty bone splinters would prick and mark my palms. How loud would I have to yell to remain unheard? Does it even matter why I'm yelling?

VI.

Not this dream again: watching her come on top of me, amazed and frightened, dusk-light like water swirls slowly into the room, hovers like perfume, and what I thought was a vision of her holding a bouquet of daisies is a mugger swinging a switchblade, I'm pinned face-down, his knees pressed on my shoulder blades, I'm slit nape to hip, kicked blind, and on a cold metal table, I can feel the delicate, deliberate tug of thread through my skin, can hear the clink and ping of the tools so clearly they must glitter and shine, like a thousand tuning forks waking me to a voice whispering *This is the only body you have.*

VII.

Reading Buson again: "A field of mustard, / no whale in sight, / the sea darkening." I believe that he has seen whales—think of it!—but not today: the ocean circles in its own abyss, over Kyoto mustard seeds thrown like snowy ash, the jolly fisherman rests his head into his hands, and his customers, ordering nothing, hunch down the alley. I lived this day. Sharon Hill, February, and after we buried B. we went to Packey's Pub, did the Irish Catholic funeral routine: shots of Bushmills, roasted pork, cigarettes, on and on till closing. Quigs pissed his pants, Chico cried. I can't remember a word. Heading home was one icy stretch of glittering dark after another, feeling a little lighter in my soft buzzing sadness, sinking through one of those rare moments of confidence when I feel myself thinking "...if I'm going to die, if that is this life, it might as well be now. I'm ready, I can do this, I'm believing this...," words blowing right through me as if they came in a letter from a friend about her last vacation that arrives almost just in time because the house has been empty for days, I haven't talked to anyone in days, she's stuck some pictures of mountains and white sands and the sea as blue as air, I thumb-tack them to the corkboard I stare at as I write this and wonder where all the beautiful people in bathing suits are now.

III

OBJECTIVE-SUBJECTIVE EXERCISE: I

Death: obligatory plurality
> —Jacques Roubaud

It was a free service. We were a journalistic enterprise. There's something to lying. One of the harder parts is knowing. Insert your story here. The fact is I'm trying to imagine this. I'm straightening my tie. I shake the man's hand sitting across from me. He hands me his obituary. He tells me he has written all four single-spaced typed pages himself. That I must run it word for word. His trench coat is tan. His hat is gray. His glasses are thick. His posture is proud. Veins emboss the bones in his hands. The skin is light brown. I smell mothballs, cigarettes, coffee, newspapers. I think no. He says I've got six months to do it. I might not be here in six months. Borges talks about how certain he is in his hope extending as long as the future. He wants new words based on the old ones. This requires hope. The examples he gives are visuals at dawn or dusk. He went blind. He offers shifts in the day's color. He likes the sky purple stretched to orange. He likes the world winding up and winding down. He says "we say 'twilight'" if we're remembering an end. He doesn't refer to mornings. The point is clear. We know we would say "dawn." He wants something specific and swooping that embraces all the senses at a moment's notice. Buenos Aires, June 14, 1926, 6:18 a.m., rain-just-stopped smell, street lamp on, trolley clank, horse trot, oranges, cold watch clicking, no one word and wanting one.

Objective-Subjective Exercise: II

I've tilted the lamp toward me because I can't quite make out the obits. Laid out in three-by-five-inch blocks across an entire fold of newspaper, some of them have photos. Take the lawyer: he looks distracted by nothing, there's reserve in his posture, in his cheekbones and lips, content in life. Light—from the flashbulb, through the photographer's studio windows, from somewhere deeper down—blankets his eyes like a cataract. I can tell they're blue. Starched shirt and pressed tie, blazer worn on weekends and vacations, he looks at his wife, back at the photographer's hand holding the clicker above the flashbulb—his head under a black sheet—and smiles so convincingly it defies the idea of absence, beams through any thought of anguish carried since birth. Some of the words are equally glorious: *loving father, devoted husband, wonderful man, esteemed colleague, skilled golfer, snappy dresser (as he liked to be called), generous tipper*—mainly two-word phrases in the third person followed with a voice stranded somewhere between active and passive: *he was..., he had been..., he was the recipient of..., for 30 years of service, he was honored with....* There's little sentence variety. I see the point. He is past tense. Verbs take their time-slowed, distance-crawl at an eye's pace across paper while his picture inhabits the form of a dome in my head. Mammoth. Saintly. Loud. Squirming particles of light. The next paragraph shifts to the present with the simple *to be* form said only once pointing toward love's abyss: *He is survived by.* Wife, sons, daughter, grandchildren, brother, sisters, even his mother still cries with the living. I wrote obits once. Only so much was allowed. The reporters would call all this nonsense. *Run what you can prove, prove what you run.* Editors called it grounds for dismissal. I'm generalizing. I'm trying to say all I can held up against all I'm forbidden to tell you. What do you think? Too direct, chatty, mannered, suffering from an impoverished concept, overdone, overly self-referential, true, false, death, resurrection, love as a noun and verb, embodied, embodying the difference between blood in the veins and outside them, what that means sometimes.

DRIVE

Let me take you by the hand, look you in the eyes to tell you how I want to climb into them again and sleep like a seed in a sleeve of milkweed, let me tell you again about the obituaries' old ink pressed in my hands, how my morning began that day five years ago when a woman came by *The Sun* to pick her husband's photo up—cancer, New Year's weekend—and all I could muster was "Sorry, I don't know where...," how her face changed forever again, utterly still and shattered, her daughter undoing and undoing the Velcro on her sneakers, how that sound clings to me like a hot breeze just passed through, always, no matter how far I drive, last lights of a city going and going on, windows down, radio blasted with Hendrix or Barber, slow traffic of fog and lilac gliding over hills dotted with hay stacks, fading silos, and two horses grazing in their eternity, tails swaying like laundry, heads bent, content in their hunger.

Note to Self

Rummaging through a pile of papers and bills, I find a note: *it doesn't even matter how good you are at it you're done doing it anyway done.* No punctuation, all one line on stationery from a small newspaper where I'd worked about two years. The handwriting is a jagged crumbling script running sort of diagonally across the page, like I was walking while I wrote, had nothing firm to lean on except my thigh or the person's back in front of me, drunk-person scribblings, words grief-stricken, something had been desperately realized or frantically captured at a wrong moment, an awkward place—in the lunch room at high-noon, during a telephone call, at the copier— an irascibly predestined epiphany, I must have uttered it to myself under my breath over and over, and re-reading it, I hear the rhythm of the words, not the words themselves:

it doesn't even matter...over-stretched iambs, stiff, indulgently Romantic, phony...

how good you are it... suddenly clipped and biting, even the smallest word—*it*—stings like a wet-towel slap, must have been a heavy day at the Obit desk for the point is this: obits are obits, one is not better than another, but some are tougher to write: the nearly unaccountable spell-check of names; substantiating phone calls to coroners, funeral directors, family members; journalist integrity pressed against the glass of the greater void that may exist finally in the mind fifteen, twenty times a day—more so around the holidays; seven dollars an hour...

you're done doing it anyway... firmly colloquial, coach-speak, I want to yell it, pound my fist with each hard accent—*an–y–way*—a loose and harsh reassurance, maybe I gave my notice that day, or for the first time I seriously considered it, ready to walk out unannounced, a subtle disappearance, "Where is he?," there were stories of old obit writers never coming back from lunch, from a smoke, from the unmentioned, I could've slipped into my car, out of one moment of immobility and into another, I could have...

done... for emphasis, I guess—it's all a guess—no period, but the end of it just the same, unintentional, the next outburst cut short and hovering, or the point slammed home and hovering....

Dr. Kevorkian's Statement to Michigan's Superior Court as Prepared by Democratic Gubernatorial Candidate Geoffrey Fieger

If you look at a leaf—say one out in the sun so long it has taken on the black freckles of a Spanish woman—and pick it up, only to watch it crumble through your fingers, then you, too, will eventually long for some form of anesthesia. You'll have earned it if you look at it correctly for the proper duration. It varies. I shouldn't have to explain this. It could be Southern Comfort on the rocks, or a chilled, black sambuca that could be mistaken for blood if the lighting is just so. I enjoy the bone-smoothing rush alcohol offers, and, though many don't know this, I smoke. Once, while I loaded some sodium pentothal into the I.V., my patient at the time, multiple sclerosis I believe, said she smelled cigarette on my sleeve; it reminded her of a boy she might have loved once in high school, and in her moment of remembering something nearly pure, she almost regretted coming to me. I wanted to say something comforting, Emersonian maybe—*Implications, my dear, implications. Closed means you may now open. At the lowest depth of dirt there lies gardenia. Illness to health, my dear, not the other way around...ask your mother. Open the blinded window for a view of the lake. Yes, you need to sit awhile to catch its stillness. Stillness, my dear, is peace and nothing else, the stillness of the earth.* This is all very good. I don't pay attention to my needs anymore.

How shall I put this? All you need to know is that what I do requires a tremendous amount of distance and control. It is how I perform well. It's like that with any job, and if you begin to identify with them, you can't do your duty. Maybe this helps. When I was serving in Korea, the colonel of my M.A.S.H. unit would sometimes, in the middle of operating, just walk out. He kept seeing his wife's and his son's arms blown off. All I do is react to the sea. He couldn't see that, the chief surgeon!

Sometimes, I weep openly at things, but I'm still invulnerable. I can act freely—no family, no big piles of money, no license to revoke—because I help widen the circle, draw new ones. I can pick leaves all day off the sidewalk, if I want. And I do. I can snap their veins and hold them up to my ear, swoon to their rustling music as they fall, like blood's lone iamb reverberating throughout its tunnels of veins, like a waterfall, and particularly today, like applause.

THE UNDERTAKER PREPARING HIS MOTHER

—for Joe Boyd Jr.

After he snaps on the thin second skin of his milky latex gloves, the silence of frozen rivers begins its hum inside her ears that only he can hear. If he's lit candles, may they shed their threads of smoke as he presses the flame into his palm, may ash drift like moths over her lips for she has inherited the gorgeous view that oceans have. May his fingers run rust's blush over her cheeks, touch shadow to her eyes, giving them their wide design, like a sky's.

MEDITATION ON PREPARATORY DEPRESSION

This is the time when the patient may just ask for a prayer, when he begins to occupy himself with things ahead rather than behind.
—Elisabeth Kübler-Ross

Deep into summer, there's little sleep. Most nights, I'm on the cusp until dawn, thick with sweat and regret. This morning, it's cicadas. They must be wringing their wings, that rapid whine of somnolence. I have no dream to forget or subconsciously argue with, no climax of a nightmare to twitch my body up, no gauzy residue of some dome-lit redemption. Repetition, the droll music of counting sheep and Hail Marys, soft murmurs of my childhood insomnia. Then forms float from trees. Some leaves falling early. Tall grass sways elegantly in a breeze's indecipherable, unmistakable weave whipped up, not by the sea sliding, but by an ambulance crying by. So much for a pastoral. Still, there must be something ideal enough I want. Coffee, cigarettes, chat by the water cooler: "Morning." "How's the weekend shaping up?" "The kids?" All that's mustered after the lags in traffic, all that's smiled through after the squeeze in, then out, of the subway like chattel. All we hide and know, denial on full throttle. Knowing where the day has gone, is going. Tomorrow, I will walk the thirty-three blocks to the Holocaust Museum. The time it will take. Dull flashes of guilt will glimmer like snowflakes at night. And after, I will hail a taxi. The driver will nod *Where to?*

Meditation on a Suicide

...if there is no difference between the sublime and the paltry, if the Son of God can undergo judgment for shit, then human existence loses its dimensions and becomes unbearably light.
—Milan Kundera

True enough. But, I still can't say how or why I would want to leave this world on my own terms.

Listening to Brubeck's "Take Five" doesn't take long, relatively speaking, and it never gets above the level of a quiet conversation, like those held in confessionals or movie theaters right after the lights dim. It's just piano, bass, and drums shuffling unvertiginously, and Desmond avoids the root all he can, his lines slipping like sunlight on a butterfly. Every time I put it on, I wait for the solos that take off, not like a wren, but a Harley or Mustang, a drunk Marine-something so American objects on shelves shiver, and then fall off. But it never happens. Maybe they were on to something with this resignation from their lives that were trying to go everywhere on four chords and five beats. But then again, they didn't resign; all they did was reject the fundamental union of improvisation, which was their lives, because they could. Like I said, I don't know. Don't trouble yourself with what it is I want.

We want to look at each other sometimes, the kind of look

that's uneasiness laced with desire, or the other way around. Around here, they're unidentical twins, so it doesn't much matter. Right now, for instance, I'm looking at Andrew Wyeth's nude Helga, *On Her Knees*. After a while, I want her, and I'm almost convinced she wants me too, except she's been looking down at a pillow all this time and her face is as flushed as bruised peaches. Her hands are behind her. I can't imagine holding them enough to go through with it. The more I look at it, the more I see that she's never been comfortable with this. So without ever touching the skin behind the ear, or kissing all the way down the inner forearm, we've turned each other down. And all this "passion," which is how Wyeth described it, is timeless. No wonder she was looking away. There's nothing like anonymity suffused with passion for all eternity. It smothers, I think, and it leavens.

I think it's all about becoming attainable, and being unattainable because there was a time when I was a part of God. I was provisionally eternal back then. I can't say for sure whether or not I liked it, but why wouldn't I? When I was seven, I told Father Donahoe how my week was going. After a cough, he gave me ten Hail Marys and ten Our Fathers. I kneeled there for forty-five minutes. My back ached. This was my privilege, to be cleansed as such. I was the last to leave chapel that day, and Sister Amadeus kept me after that to clap out the erasers, punishment for failure in small Catholic towns. I found out that taking the Lord's name in vain also involved singing "fuck-shit-damn, fuck-shit-damn" to the tune of "Three Blind

Mice" to no one in particular. B. told me this. He walked me through shit for years. We were taught that God was in the details, that we were made in God's image. I know I'm wrong, but I sit down and try to figure out a way to become attainable to God again. Nothing, so far, has been deemed acceptable, or worked, for that matter.

B. grew up one town over from me. They're both unacceptable towns to be raised in, unless you're a Catholic, or at least Episcopalian. Even then, it might not do any good. When B. went and shot himself in front of St. Joe's, where we were baptized, the pigeons in the eaves flew off in every direction, like veins and arteries or the lines on a map. The sky held still behind all this. That was his way out, and I'll love him for it. I'd better because I'm scared to death for him. It is God's nature to reject what was once a part of him. So what does that make B.? Oh, not now Whitman. I still love you, but please not today. Every single morning, at 6:30, pigeons fly out of those eaves when Mrs. McMurtry presses the bass pedals on the organ with her feet, as if she were walking through mud. Every blessed morning, and, occasionally, when I hear that unseemly shudder of surprise in some pigeons' clutter of wings, I feel closer to the truth than anyone.

STEPPING INTO POETRY

—after Gerald Stern

Here's what you would give to lose your pitiful dreams with B. tapping the cold window with a revolver and laughing, leaving your coffee and bagel and books on the table with the asphodels and following him out to the field and sobbing the whole long walk, your thickening dreams of snow falling on the cherry mess of his head, your soul-clenching dreams of traveling once more with your brother, this time on a dirt bike through the Mojave, the Pacific always there and never, ever closer. You're swearing this time you'd give it all up to return to the stained and wobbly tables, to have your books again be yours again, your lucky pen and life, the little stars and dog ears of paper, the cold coffee to sip and not scowl over, if only you could hear some laughs and applause as if you were approaching, your name, to be there and shake the hands of all your living and dead, to feel the applause and cheers of that small crowd seep through you like a drug.

Meditation on Denial & Isolation

I.

I nod for coffee, and the diner table wobbles a little as I rest
my head in my hand. In my other hand four sparrows quarrel
over the crusts of bread B. has tucked in it. He's laughing.
Apparently, his death is no different from a star's—implosion
and light for at least a million years. When he asks for water,
I go get it; when he drinks, it runs over his chin to his white
oxford shirt. *Now go get me a smoke* is what I hear, so I do
that too. *I loved doing this,* and he blows three halos the size
of beer cans. Since he is here, I ask him what love is. *A river
in childhood when you're not a child anymore,* punches me
in the arm, *Wuss.* I ask him what he is now. *Depends. Bad
days, for you, a cyclonic vision of salt braided over the eyes of
your wife, who's bald from chemo. Good days, I'm a familiar
name with some photographs...*The bell on the counter dings
and someone else gets their coffee or Key lime pie. I stand up
and pay, sleepy.

II.

Moonblind is what Ground Control called Aldrin after he kept
saying *Sea of Tranquility* over and over for an hour straight.
Isolated, he compensated with a litany. *Sea of Tranquility;
au revoir* for the air strapped to his back; *affaire d'amour*

for those of us doing circles on the blue-eyed marble he'd slip behind his thumbnail. Many young men, with all sorts of shapely eyes, right around that time, were struck with the familiar look of puzzlement as bullets whisked through them, as if no one were there to stop their trajectory. Rice paddies, mines, LBJ, Pol Pot, Tricky Dick. Whatever works, Buzz. Keep them coming: data fata secutus; clarum et venerabile nomen; Gott mit uns; che sara, sara; zoe mou, sas agapo!

On Two Scenes from *The Deer Hunter*

I.

Because B.'s a line break that hasn't come yet. Simply because. Because grief stills his image, his image that breaks like a silver wave or a blue vase on a gray marble floor. I will always have words to fall back on, though they're rarely right. They form after they shatter in the eye and ear. But my *grief's* purpose? To recover a white beach's fleeting panache and wash, to piece together an indigo vase shattered and shimmering, to get to the line that never breaks too soon, as if it were in a script composed under this winter sky...? No. I can't explain grief. It is its own end.

II. "God Bless America"

One of the last frames stills the gang over scrambled eggs and beer, a full-room shot of those who've remained, more or less. "God Bless America," and at the end Cimino zooms in on Streep, who, for a moment, smiles before memory turns on her and changes her face into that side-glance of grief directed at no one, nothing, the floor. Light shrouds her, and, for a minute, while it's wrong, I'm in love. Then, a guitar I see in blues and grays. Her glance hovers. The tape rewinds. The TV turns to snow. The glance, the guitar, the light blue twitching across the floor flashes above my eyes, flecked and flowing, never the same way twice.

This is the grieving mind in memory, a white hush, the guitar's ellipses and the ellipses of stars gathering outside, which I don't see right now, but remember well enough, when I imagine them stuck in a sky that's plain and dark.

III. ROULETTE

Somewhere in the middle of the film DeNiro's Michael returns, says *Take care* to his friend's wife, who's long since been trapped in her dread, mute with cyclones of imagination, what some may call a lack of closure. This friend, her husband, loses his legs to Charlie and the Red River, lives in a VA hospital now, doesn't want to leave because *it's like a resort; they've got bowlin' and basketball.* A third friend, AWOL, plays russian roulette in a Saigon basement. He dies. There's nothing involuntary. There's nothing subtle. It has to be. DeNiro brings him home. And later, because they can't speak to each other, they sing. If no one's home, I cry and cry and cry.

IV.

What do you want me to say? Go ahead. I deserve, like you, to be judged. Let me say that I evolve to infancy, that it's self-inflicted, that I'm grasping at the unreachable root tip of suffering, image and after-image, free from harm, welcoming pain, gazing astonished into the mutable past, into a foreseeable future that transcends its identical twin: a stare of bewildered infatuation with the present. It's only dangerous because the stares so closely resemble each other.

Last summer I went back to Sharon Hill and, to tell the truth, I'm not sure what I went looking for. I visited a church, but I didn't go in. I didn't have to because a friend killed himself on the steps of it. You almost know his name. You know this already. And though I like to repeat myself, it is tiresome for me too, like wind. He was baptized in that church, knew nothing of that day except from pictures and the little sky-blue folder holding the certificate in the sacristy. Bland declarative sentences. Catholics. Too many times he turned the other cheek from himself and found, waiting there, himself. He didn't talk about doing it. It's none of my business. Now he's mine. Now he's a line break that's taken me years to get to.

MEDITATION ON ACCEPTANCE

The jonquils she asked me to move to the back are beginning to take to the light now on a steady basis, despite how cool it's been lately. I didn't want to do it at first, but then I remembered how she used to kiss my neck as she grabbed my nape, and that small ascension of freesia from her wrist. Green stem, brown leaves around it on the ground. This dirt, that dirt. Light here, light there. Water running in the hair-pin roots, in the clouds, in the shadows of clouds, and for maybe millions of years blood has surrounded our lungs without flooding them, hardly ever.

The other day felt like the last day I'd ever have the pleasure of watching the pointless flurry of traffic from a diner booth. Don't ask. Call it quiet expectation, hearty narcissism. The waitress said to me, "Here you are, sugar...now you're set." She snapped me from my old daydream, the hospital one: surrounded by narcissi—sweetness, bobbysoxers, quail, pequenitas—my brother and I have snapped and stuck some bellsongs behind our ears. A Captain and Coke sweats on the tray in front of me. We've turned to listen to the music of sprinklers clicking on like typewriters beginning a new line. He's tapping his pool stick on the floor and I'm tossing the cue ball hand to hand, looking out the window. I must have something. Sky hangs, cool and pink, like a sliced grapefruit, a blood orange. The a.m. radio crackles with August lightning storms...always nearly morning ... occasional swell of rain and wind. Ghosts work hard, like grape gleaners, in the curtains. What they sing remains nameless, close, and though my brother's here to say goodbye, I'm not afraid.

That happens when the waitress calls me back into the light here, not there. So I say, "Well, thanks. I guess I'm set...," the sort of lie that reaches around morality and time to prick the soul. To get what she wanted, she didn't have to say a word. What I owe stares back in ink.

Could it be that what moves us is distance?

Coltrane's "Psalm, Part 4" rises and falls like the scent of bellsong, sweetness, and sundial arranged on an altar. He found a way to let it pass through him like light and lust and dust and grief.

To meet him, I can't wait.

Notes

The lines quoted from Wallace Stevens in "To the Girl in the Second Row" are from his poems "The Idea of Order at Key West" and "To an Old Philosopher in Rome."

"On a Meeting of Philip Levine and Larry Levis" is modeled after Levine's poem "On the Meeting of Garcia Lorca and Hart Crane."

"In Memory of William Matthews" gets, in part, its title from Matthews' poem "In Memory of W. H. Auden," which, in turn, gets its title from Auden's "In Memory of W. B. Yeats."

Buson's haiku that appears in "After Andrew Wyeth's *Whale Rib*" is Robert Hass's translation.

Borges' words in "Objective-Subjective Exercise: II" come from his essay "Immortality."

At the end of "Meditation on Denial & Isolation," the following phrases are loosely translated into:

— "data fata secutus," from the Latin, "Following what is
    decreed by fate"
— "clarum et venerabile nomen," from the Latin, "An
illustrious and venerable name"
— "Got mit uns," from the German, "God with us"

— "che sara, sara," from the Italian, "what will be, will be"
— "zoe mou, sas agapo," from the Greek, "my life, I love you," also quoted in Byron's "Maid of Athens, Ere We Part"